Miss Thackery
and the Bee

Story by Pauline Cartwright
Illustrated by Coral Tulloch

PM Plus Chapter Books

Emerald

U.S. Edition © 2013 HMH Supplemental Publishers
10801 N. MoPac Expressway
Building #3
Austin, TX 78759
www.hmhsupplemental.com

9 10 11 12   1957   14
18649

Text: Pauline Cartwright
Illustrations: Coral Tulloch
Printed in China by 1010 Printing International Ltd

Miss Thackery and the Bee

ISBN 978 0 75 784115 6

Contents

CHAPTER 1

The Class Show

Jaron's class put on a show for the class next door. Amber and Colin sang a song. Kane spelled ten very long words. Kirsty did a magic trick. Everyone had thought of something they were good at and then performed a small item.

Jaron played the piano. He played a song he had learned with his music teacher, Miss Thackery. Everyone was surprised by how well he played and they clapped hard. Jaron was so pleased his face felt hot!

Jaron loved music. One day, his father had promised him, he could learn the guitar. After that he could try the clarinet. But first he had to learn music on the piano that Grandma had left them.

Jaron remembered his grandma playing. Her fingers had rippled and bounced on the keys. Her body had swayed in time to the music.

"Everything you learn for the piano will be useful for other instruments," his dad said.

So Jaron worked at his piano practice. One day he wanted to be a musician in a band.

Sometimes Jaron thought that the music he learned from Miss Thackery wasn't very exciting. He would let the songs Grandma had played sing in his head. Then bits of Grandma's music seemed to come out of his fingers as he touched the keys.

"Is that what you're supposed to be playing?" His mom would ruffle his hair as she passed.

"I'm just playing this for fun. It helps me remember Grandma."

"Great," his mom would smile. "But remember to do your lesson practice as well."

CHAPTER 2

Piano Lesson

Every Tuesday afternoon, Jaron emptied his homework and lunchbox out of his backpack and put his music inside. Then his mother drove him to the Apple Row Apartments where Miss Thackery lived and taught music.

One Tuesday Jaron's mom glanced at him as they pulled up outside the apartment block.

"You're very quiet, Jaron. Are you feeling all right?" she asked him.

He didn't feel sick but his stomach had the same nervous feeling that he always felt when he arrived for his piano lesson. He didn't know how to explain it.

So he just said, "I'm fine."

"Play well for Miss Thackery," said his mom. "I'll pick you up when your lesson is over."

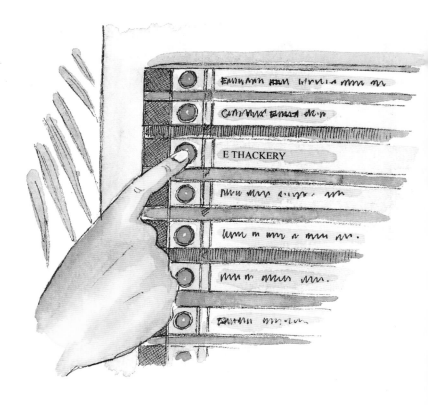

E THACKERY

As he climbed the five wide, white steps his heart began to beat a little faster. He reached out to the plate with all the tenants' names and pressed the buzzer labeled E THACKERY. His heart beat a little faster still.

Inside, Miss Thackery would be checking his image on a screen. Suddenly her voice, through the small grill on the wall, said, "Come up, Jaron." The doorlatch clicked. Jaron pushed open the door. Then he pushed it shut behind him.

While he rode the elevator to # 28, SECOND FLOOR, Jaron tried to smile. He breathed in and out slowly to stop his heart from beating so fast. He didn't want Miss Thackery to know that he was scared of her.

CHAPTER 3
Miss Thackery

Miss Thackery was tall and thin. She sat very straight on the chair beside Jaron. When Jaron played well, Miss Thackery said, "Good" in a brisk sort of way. She waved one hand in time with Jaron's music.

Sometimes Jaron thought that her long, thin fingers might slap his hands if he made mistakes. But they never did.

It was the look on her face that made Jaron imagine they might. It was the way she always smiled with her lips together. It was because he had never heard her laugh. It was because she never talked about anything except the music lesson. When he made a mistake she simply said, "Again."

Once or twice she had asked, "Do you like this tune, Jaron?" Even when he didn't, Jaron said, "Yes, Miss Thackery." Sometimes Miss Thackery said, "You played well, Jaron." She smiled her closed-lips smile. Sometimes she said, "More practice this week, Jaron."

Jaron did love music and he wanted to learn all that he could. But when he was in the elevator, leaving Miss Thackery's, he always felt glad that his hour with her was over.

CHAPTER 4

Changing Tunes?

"I want to change my music teacher," Jaron told his mom and dad.

"Why?" asked Dad.

"I'm scared of her," he said.

"Why?" said Mom.

"I just am." Jaron didn't know how to explain his feelings.

He watched his mom look at his dad. Then they both looked back at him. He knew they were trying very hard to understand.

Dad asked, "Are you finding the music too hard? Does Miss Thackery give you pieces that you find too difficult to play?"

"No," Jaron replied.

"There must be some reason for you to feel scared," said his mother, looking concerned.

"Does Miss Thackery get angry with you?"

"No," said Jaron.

"Well, what is it that makes you scared?" asked Dad.

Jaron tried hard to explain how he felt. "She never smiles properly, and she never talks to me."

Dad looked at Mom again. Then he said to Jaron, "Well, you're not really there to talk a lot. You're there to learn music."

"Dad's right, Jaron. And as well as being just a nice person who wouldn't like to know that you were scared of her, Miss Thackery is a very good music teacher," said Mom. She put an arm around Jaron. "Now how about playing that tune you played in the show at school?"

"Yes," agreed Dad. "Play that tune that everybody liked."

Mom and Dad clapped when he had finished playing.

"Now play one of Grandma's tunes," smiled Mom. Jaron wished Miss Thackery smiled like his mom and dad.

CHAPTER 5

The Bee!

One afternoon Jaron had to wait after he had pushed the buzzer at Apple Row Apartments. When Miss Thackery finally answered, she sounded different.

Jaron stepped out of the elevator and into her apartment. Miss Thackery wasn't there. Then she called out.

He followed her voice. Miss Thackery was wrapped in a red blanket. What was the matter with her, wondered Jaron.

"There's a bee! There's a bee!"

"Pardon?" said Jaron.

"A bee! In the room!"

Jaron heard a buzzing at the window. He saw a bee batting its body against the window pane. Surely Miss Thackery wasn't frightened of a bee!

"Do you want me to put the bee outside, Miss Thackery?"

"Oh, could you! *Please*!"

She was frightened. Very frightened. Frightened of one itsy-bitsy bee! The window was open, but the bee couldn't find its way out.

"I need something to catch the bee, Miss Thackery." Miss Thackery gave a small squeak of fright.

"Can I get a glass from your kitchen?"

She nodded.

There was a postcard on her refrigerator, held there by a magnet. Jaron picked that up, too.

"Jaron?"

"I'm coming, Miss Thackery."

CHAPTER 6

Jaron to the Rescue!

As Miss Thackery watched and made more frightened noises, Jaron put the glass over the bee. The bee buzzed even more angrily. Jaron slid the postcard between the glass and the window pane.

"Got you!" he said, lifting the glass, with its postcard lid, away from the window.

Jaron moved the bee-trap to the window opening. He tipped it forward and slid the postcard away. The bee flew off over the city, far away.

"It's gone now, Miss Thackery."

Jaron realized his heart wasn't beating as fast today. He didn't feel even a tiny bit frightened. Yet the scary Miss Thackery, tall, thin, never-a-hair-out-of-place Miss Thackery, had been frightened – of a bee!

Miss Thackery dropped the blanket and came into the room. Her hair was messed up. Her face was still red.

"Oh thank you, Jaron!" She smiled, really smiled, so that her teeth showed. Jaron thought she looked quite pretty. Mom and Dad were right. She was a perfectly nice person.

Once he never would have dared, but now he asked, "Miss Thackery, why are you scared of bees?"

"I'm allergic to bees," explained Miss Thackery. "If I get stung, I become ill very quickly. I could die if I don't get the right medication."

CHAPTER 7

A New Tune

"And then," Jaron told his parents later, "we had some milk and cookies."

"A perfectly nice person," smiled Mom.

"We told you," said Dad.

"Then she asked me to play any song I liked," said Jaron. "I played one of Grandma's. She liked it and she showed me how to put in the bass chords that I hadn't been able to work out on my own."

"Great!" said Mom.

"And then, do you know what she played?" Jaron asked his parents. "Part of a song called 'Flight of the Bumble Bee'."

Mom, Dad, and Jaron laughed and laughed.

"It's really cool music – just like a bee," said Jaron. "Miss Thackery said she might teach it to me one day."

"So you think you might like to keep going to your lessons with Miss Thackery?" asked Dad.

"Of course," said Jaron. He couldn't remember now why he had ever been frightened of her.

"Anyway, she needs someone like you around now and then," said Mom, "in case another bee gets inside."

"I suppose so," smiled Jaron.